AMAZINGLY, AWESOME SNAILS!

By K.S. Tankersley

Little John Publishing
Glendale, AZ

Little John Publishing, a Division of Southwest
Training Development, Inc.,
20118 N. 67th Avenue, Ste. 300-159
Glendale, AZ 85308, U.S.A.

Paperback ISBN 13: 978-1497367043
and ISBN 10: 1497367042

Library of Congress Cataloging-in-Publication Data

Tankersley, K.S.
Amazingly, Awesome Snails!/K.S. Tankersley
  ISBN 13: 978-1497367043 and ISBN 10: 1497367042

Has anyone ever told you to "stop moving like a snail?" when they wanted you to hurry up? If so, then you are in good company. People have been comparing things to the small and slow moving snail for centuries. Here is your chance to learn more about this amazing and awesome creature!

The History of Snails

Snails can be found both on the land and in water depending on their type.

Snails belong to a group of animals called mollusks. The snail is related to clams, mussels, squid, oysters and the octopus. Mollusks have unsegmented, soft-bodied, spineless creatures. Their soft bodies are protected by hard shells of various shapes and sizes.

The word "mollusk" comes from Latin and means "soft nut." Mollusks belong to the class

Gastropodo or gastropods. The

word "gastro" means "belly" and
"pod" means "foot" so their
name is "belly foot" which refers
to the large foot which takes up
much of their body.

Scientists believe that this
group of animals first appeared
in the ocean over 600 million
years ago before fish, lobsters

and even whales appeared on the earth.

Characteristics of Snails

The body of a snail is long, moist and shiny with a shell to protect its soft body. When the snail feels in danger, it pulls itself back into its shell and seals itself with a layer of slime.

Many species of snail have a plate on the bottom of the snail's foot called an "operculum" which seals the shell closed when the snail has retreated inside.

There are over 40,000 species of snails in the world. The smallest species is the size of a pinhead, while the largest, the Australian Trumpet Snail can grow to about 2.5 feet (80 cm) long. Although people are more familiar with the land snails, there are actually more species of marine snails than there are land dwelling snails.

Snails live in gardens, in trees and forests, in ponds and even in the ocean. They are found all over the earth and live anywhere that they can find shade and a moist climate that can keep their soft skin from drying out.

The majority of snails has lungs and breathes air but there are other types of snails that have gills and breathe like fish in water. Whether the snail has lungs or gills is more dependent on the type of snail it is rather than whether it lives on land or in the water.

Generally, snails like warm, moist locations. This type of climate keeps them from drying out. Snails like to come out when it is fairly dark or overcast and the air is moist. They prefer to be active during times when there is heavy dew or warm, soft

rain in the area. The sun can dry out their body and cause them to die. The snail will also pull its body back into its shell and seal itself with slime to prevent water loss and drying out. Snails avoid going out in the bright, direct sunlight whenever possible due to this risk of dehydration and death.

The Snail's Body

The name "snail" comes from the German word "snahhan" which means "to creep." Snails cover about 30 feet or 10 meters in an hour when they are steadily moving. The snail's large foot muscle moves in waves to move the snail on the ground. Backward waves of the foot muscle move the snail forward with the slime helping to reduce surface friction. Some types of snails are known to "gallop" by

arching the front end of its foot
forward while the tail half glides
ahead with backward waves.

The snail puts slime on the
foot to help it move and provide
some protection from friction and
sharp surfaces to the foot as it
moves across surfaces. The slime
leaves a shiny, slime trail behind
the moving snail. If you look

carefully, you can see the slime trail on the surface of where the snail has moved. The snail uses both slime and suction to hold itself on surfaces such as trees or leaves. It can also wrap its foot

around a small branch to help itself climb up a branch to reach the leaves. The slime comes out from the front and hardens after it is exposed to the air. You can often see a shiny path on the surface of where a snail has been when the sun lights up the hardened slime still remaining the surface.

Snails are plant eaters. They cannot bite or chew but instead, use their ribbon-like tongue, called a radula, to scrape the food and put it into its mouth. The tongue has teeth which help the snail scrape off small bits of the leaf when it is eating. Snails eat mostly living plants but will also eat decaying plants, fruits and soft plant bark, vegetables, fungi and algae. Some species

can cause damage to crops so
farmers may consider them pests.

Snails that live in water eat algae
and microscopic creatures that
are found on the surface of water
weeds. They scrape their food off
with their rough tongues just like
land snails do.

Most species of land snail have four tentacles on its head. The snail's eyes are usually located on the top two tentacles which are usually longer than the bottom two tentacles.

Although the snail has eyes, scientists believe that the snail's eyes do not see very well. They think snails can only sense light and darkness. Light sensors on the lips, foot, and mantle help the snail find dark places in which to hide and stay moist. The snail uses its bottom set of tentacles to tap the ground much like a blind person with a tapping cane feels the ground in front of them. The snail uses its smaller set of tentacles for smell and to feel its way around. The smaller set of tentacles may also be able to sense vibrations in the environment around them to warn them of danger.

The snail has a primitive brain. It is able to learn from experience and conditioning.

The snail's mouth is located on the bottom of its head near the tentacles. The majority of its internal organs are located inside the shell where the shell is largest. This is known as the visceral hump. Here you will find the snail's stomach, kidney, heart, liver, lung, and mantle.

The snail's anus is located on the top of the snail's body just behind the breathing hole or respiratory pore. While this may seem an odd place to expel waste, the snail releases feces or poop only when they are exhaling. The feces are wrapped in a clear, bag-like membrane which protects the snail from the waste.

The shell of a land snail is made up mostly of calcium carbonate. The shell only grows as long as the snail has a good diet full of calcium. If it does not get this rich supply of calcium, the shell will grow soft and begin to crack.

The spirals of most snail shells grow in a clockwise direction which means that it always coils to the right. This type of shell is called a *dextral* shell. A few species of snails have left-handed shells, called *sinistral* shells. These shells coil and grow counter-clockwise.

Snail Predators

Snails do not bite, sting or scratch. Instead, their only source of protection is their hard shell. The shell offers the snail protection against predators such as rats, mice, birds, crows, badgers, foxes, moles and other larger snails. They can also be preyed upon by beetles, frogs, ducks, snakes or even lizards while on land. Although the hard shell protects the snail from many predators, some are able to

bite through the hard shell with
their powerful teeth.

In the water, crabs, fish,
whales and even other larger
snails have been known to prey
on smaller snails.

People are also a threat to the
snail. People in many countries
consider the snail a very special
delicacy and love to eat them.
People have created many special

recipes to serve snails at meals in tasty ways.

Snail Mating

Snails have both male and female body parts within them. They can produce both sperm and eggs themselves. To fertilize the eggs, however, they need to exchange sperm with another snail.

When snails are between 1 to 2 years old, depending upon the

species, they will bond with
another snail, usually in the
summer. Before mating, the two
snails will go through a special
courtship dance for many hours.

During this ritual, one of the
snails shoots a special dart into
the other snail's body. When this
happens, the second snail will

retreat into its shell. If it comes back out in a few minutes, the mating will continue. If it does not, the first snail will continue to look for another mate. Scientists believe that this is nature's way of making sure that the two snail species are compatible for mating. It is also believed that people got the idea of being shot with "cupid's arrow" when referring to two people falling in love.

When the two snails have determined that they are compatible mates, they twist themselves around each other and cover themselves in frothy slime. They exchange sperm sacs to fertilize their own eggs. The sperm sacs can be stored inside the snail's body for up to a year if conditions to lay the eggs are not right.

Each snail then finds a place where they can dig in the soft ground to lay their eggs in a nest located 2.5 to 4 centimeters deep. Each snail can lay about 85 to 100 eggs. The snail pushes the

eggs out from an opening behind the head. The snail covers the eggs with dirt, mucus and feces. Depending on the warmth and moisture in the soil, the eggs can hatch in 2 to 4 weeks. Mature snails may lay eggs as often as once a month or every 6 weeks when the weather is warm and damp. The most active months for snail egg laying are February through October depending on the temperature and moisture found in the region.

When the weather is warm and moist, the eggs will begin to change color within 2 weeks. The soft shells surrounding the babies will begin to fall away. The baby is born with its own soft, thin shell. The baby snail begins to eat his own eggshell as well as the other empty eggshells it finds in the nest. After the first few days, it stays in the nest and eats the tiny plants, leaves and egg shell parts it finds there.

After 4 days, the hatchling leaves the nest and continues to search for food in its environment. The shell continues to grow as the baby snail finds food to eat. After 2 weeks, the shell begins to change color. It also gets stronger and harder. The shell begins to curl around in the spiral shape as it grows. Each turn of the spiral is called a whorl.

After about 6 months, the snail's color change is complete and it has about 3 whorls on its shell. At this age, the baby is still only about half the size of the parent.

At 9 months of age, the baby snail has 4 whorls on its shell and its color is deepening to what it will be as an adult.

After the snail grows to full, adult size, the shell no longer grows larger but becomes harder and thicker. An adult snail has both an outer and an inner shell. The inner shell is strong and hard while the outer layer is thin and almost transparent. Both shells provide the protection the snail will need to protect it from predators of all types.

Life Expectancy of a Snail

While different species of snails have different life expectancies, most snails live somewhere between 3-4 years in the natural environment. Snails have been known to live up to 7-8 years but this is more unusual. Snails living in a protected environment where there are no dangers to their survival, such as in an aquarium, have been known to live up to 15 years.

When the weather is colder, snails often group together in a dark, damp, leafy area such as under rocks, piles of wet leaves or moss to hibernate. The warm rains and higher temperatures of spring will bring them out of hibernation and back into their environment. When the snails come out, the cycle of life will begin again.